Daddy's Reminders

A Black Father's Message to His Daughter

Rashid Faisal, Ed. M.

Black Ivy Scholar Publications

Detroit

Daddy's Reminders

A Black Father's Message to His Daughter

First Edition, First Printing

Printed in the United States of America

Front Cover Illustration and Design: Christie Dolar-Faisal

Book Design: Christie Dolar-Faisal

13-Digit ISBN #:9780692224717

10-Digit ISBN #:0692224718

To Grandpa Charles E. Jackson, Sr.

CONTENTS

Daddy's Reminders

Acknowledgments

First and foremost, I want to thank my wife Christie for standing beside me throughout my career in education and in authoring this book. Most of my writing occurred in the evening, on weekends, while on vacation, and other times inconvenient to my family. I am very appreciative of her love and understanding in my quest to pen my thoughts. I also thank my high-spirited daughter, Gabrielle, who is the inspiration for my writing a book on the core family values I hope she will embrace during her journey through life.

Thanks to all my friends for sharing my struggle when starting this project and following with support and encouragement when it seemed too difficult to be completed. Words cannot express my gratitude for a countless number of friends who applauded my decision to pen a message of guidance, hope, and inspiration for my daughter. Without the enthusiasm shown by so many family members and friends, this book may not have been written.

Apart from my efforts, the success of any project depends entirely on God. I take this opportunity to express my love and gratitude to God who is the primary reason I am successful in completing this book.

Introduction

Dr. Martin Luther King, Jr. said, "One of the greatest problems of mankind is that we suffer from poverty of the spirit which stands in glaring contrast to our scientific and technological abundance." [1] He went on to say, "The richer we have become materially, the poorer we have become morally and spiritually."[2] I agree wholeheartedly with Dr. King's statement. We are rapidly becoming a nation with little or no regard for spiritual and moral values. As fathers we must work together to restore spiritual and moral values in the African American community.

Dr. Robert M. Franklin, past-president of Morehouse College and author of *Crisis in the Village: Restoring Hope in African American Communities*, made a very telling statement I deem worth sharing: "The love, nurture, mentoring, and discipline that children require are in the hands of parents and other steady and sturdy ordinary souls in the community." [3] Dr. Franklin is correct in pointing out the role of mature, responsible adults in raising healthy African American children. Children raised in stable homes have a far greater chance of growing into positive and productive adults than children raised in home environments characterized by parental irresponsibility, unhealthy relationships, and family dysfunction.

One of the defining characteristics of stable families is their use of family values to teach moral discipline to its members. There is a traditional African American saying, *"We measure good things by the length of time they will be good."*

Parents and other adult members in the African American community play critical roles in helping our children distinguish between temporary values (values with-little-or-no-lasting use) and permanent values (values good over the duration of a lifetime).

"It never faileth," is an African American proverb used by our ancestors to help African American children distinguish between permanent values and temporary ones. For example, if we are willing to be honest, the African American community and society in general value pre-marital sex over sex within marriage. How else can we explain the high percentage of African American children born outside of wedlock? How else can we explain the popularity of recreational sex in the African American community and in the larger society? Pre-marital sex is valued over waiting to have sex until marriage. Marriage is no longer highly prized. As a consequence, traditional family structures are on the decline. The impact on the African American community is troublesome.

This was not always the case in the African American community. Even during slavery when African Americans could not legally marry, marriage was valued and sought after by our enslaved ancestors. One of the most depressing characteristics of slavery was the breakup of families. In slave narratives I read, the unifying theme is spirit-breaking loss of a wife, husband, child, or another family member being sold.

Even during troublesome years of Jim Crow, the African American community valued marriage and two-parent households. Marriage and family traditionally served as institutions to provide African American children with love, nurturance, safety, intellectual guidance, financial support, and, most importantly, moral discipline and training. Unfortunately, the decline in traditional African American family structure contributes to our children searching for identity, love, and acceptance from gangs or anti-social groups. Our children are no longer receiving moral discipline and training in the home. Instead, they are learning temporary values from immature peers, entertainers, movies, videos, and music. Our children are receiving their moral education from social media and the entertainment industry.

School is a place where African American children struggle not only academically, but morally. Regrettably, the African American community relies exclusively on school to educate our children. There is a saying, *"A child only educated at school is not an educated child."* I agree with this statement and will go one step further and say, *"School is not the place for teaching moral values; it is the place where moral values are reinforced."* Moral discipline and training is best taught in the home under the care and guidance of mature, morally responsible parents and other trusted adults. The African American home is the best place to teach our children moral values.

The moral values practiced in the African American community during our most troubling periods in America are enduring in quality. Found within traditional African American marriage and family is moral values that *"never faileth."* In other words, traditional African American values provided our children with self-identity and prepared them for marriage, family, responsible parenthood, and positive membership in the community. These values helped us establish stable African American communities. Can we establish stable African American communities in absence of stable families? Can we establish stable families in absence of married, two-parent households? Can we raise healthy, productive, morally upright children in absence of stable family relationships and moral training?

Dr. Robert M. Franklin makes a very important point on the importance of stable, nurturing families to raising healthy African American children: *"Black children, like all children, thrive best when their married biological parents rear them. But when that is not possible, they can do well in other family forms so long as they are loved, supported financially, and given the safest, most nurturing environment possible."* [4] It goes without saying all children thrive best when raised by their married, biological parents in a household characterized by healthy, stable, loving relationships. There are more than a few positive examples in African American history of African American families successfully raising healthy, productive African American children.

Daddy's Reminders: A Black Fathers' Message to His Daughter is greatly influenced by my research on an African American family residing in Chandler, Oklahoma during the early decades of the 1900s. The Ellis family, headed by Whit Ellis, an African American entrepreneur and restaurant owner, and Maggie Ellis, his wife and business partner, raised ten morally upright, college-educated children during a period in history when few Americans of any color graduated from high school.[5]

Between 1920 and 1960, Whit and Maggie Ellis produced a family of ten college graduates, with eight of the children earning master's degrees and two earning doctorate degrees. The Ellis family's children earned eight bachelor degrees from historically black Langston University; bachelor's degree from historically black Wilberforce University, and University of Michigan; five master's degrees from University of Michigan, two from New Mexico University, one from historically black Prairie View University, and one from Wayne State University; and, one Ph.D. from University of Michigan, and one from Tulsa University.[4] An amazing accomplishment for any family regardless of race or socioeconomic status.

How did Whit and Maggie Ellis raise a family of ten college graduates during the oppressive era of Jim Crow segregation? A critical factor contributing to this amazing feat is inspiration for *Daddy's Reminders: A Black Father's Message to His Daughter.* The Ellis parents, while encouraging their children's college aspirations, believed in providing their children with moral discipline and training. I believe the Ellis parents' commitment to moral education is primary reason their children achieved academic success.

The Ellis family's commitment to marriage, family, self-improvement, and moral living is capsulated in "The Ellis Family's Core Values." These values were taken from Ellis family oral history compiled by Mel Chatman, the son of Margrett Ann

Ellis.[7] "The Ellis Family's Core Values" were established by Whit and Maggie Ellis as guiding principles for helping their children lead positive and productive adult lives. According to Mel Chatman, these core family values included belief in God, moral living, gaining knowledge through learning, on-going attention to self-improvement, self-respect, teamwork, and using one's full potential in accomplishing any task.[8] The Ellis family core family values assisted each child in becoming positive and productive adults.

During my reading of Ellis family history, the image of the mythical Sankofa bird kept coming to mind. This mythical bird flies forward with its head turned backward; it is symbolic of the Akan belief in the past serving as a guide for planning the future. I believe we can address social and family problems in African American communities by *re-connecting* with traditional African American values. These values sustained us during the darkest days of slavery and the hopeless hours of Jim Crow segregation. One of the things I admire most about the Ellis family is their commitment to family. Even if the Ellis children had not achieved a remarkable record of academic excellence, the core family values taught by Whit and Maggie Ellis contributed to each child becoming a successful adult.

The most critical reader of the Ellis' family history will find a family embodying the best traditions in African American marriage, family formation, and child rearing practice. There would be many more examples if the subject of positive African American family life received more than occasional attention from scholars and researchers of African American history.

Daddy's Reminders: A Black Father's Message to His Daughter represents my small contribution to the topic of using traditional African American values raise healthy, productive African American children.

Father's Impact on Daughters

Daddy's Reminders: A Black Father's Message to His Daughter is written for Black men—whether married, contemplating marriage, divorced, acting as stepfathers, unmarried with children, or serving as surrogate fathers. Dr. Robert M. Franklin said the following which plainly captures why Black fathers must lead the charge in teaching the moral values we want our children to embrace. He stated: *"If the village elders don't step up, the village idiots will."* [9] The current moral crisis in African American youth culture is the direct result of "village idiots" and "idiots outside the village" teaching our children immoral, unhealthy, unproductive, and, in some cases, criminal values.

As men and gatekeepers of the community, we must play an active role in providing moral discipline and training to our children. Too often we have given women the primary responsibility of providing our children with moral training. Early-childhood and early-adolescence are the periods when the foundations for responsible adulthood are established. It is the period when moral training is most effective. Sadly, it is during this critical period in child development when Black fathers are either absent from the lives of their children or not actively engaged in providing moral instruction. It is of critical importance Black fathers take on the primary role in providing African American children with moral training. If we neglect to do so, other less-qualified, less-suitable, and some with ill-intentions, will teach our children wrong values.

As a father, I take comfort in 3 John 4, which states, *"I have no greater joy than to hear that my children walk in truth."* We required as fathers to help our children discover the best moral values leading to healthy and productive living. I believe the moral values followed by our African American ancestors during the darkest hours of slavery and Jim Crow segregation are the best values. Embracing these moral values consistently led to positive outcomes for African American families. We must teach these moral values to our children.

Black fathers must play an active role in raising their daughters. Our daughters need as much love and support as our sons, if not more. We cannot neglect their moral discipline and training for obvious reasons. The absence of intelligent, family-oriented, morally upright Black men in the lives young African American girls is producing devastating social consequences for African American communities. Fatherless daughters are more at-risk for school failure, dropping out of school, engaging in illicit sex, teen pregnancy, alcohol and drug abuse, involvement in abusive relationships, and low-self-esteem.

We must accept the critical role we play in shaping the self-image of our daughters. Our daughters need our emotional support and moral guidance as they grow and develop from immature girls to morally responsible woman. Too many young African American girls engage in irresponsible sexual behaviors because of their yearning for father figures. We are responsible for teaching our daughters to respect their bodies and how to manage their sexuality. We must exercise *zero-tolerance* for males emotionally abusing or sexually exploiting our daughters. Can we build stable families if our community is overrun by irresponsible sexual behavior? Sexual recklessness and lack of commitment to marriage and family are primary factors contributing to the growing number of fatherless homes.

The strength of our families and the health of our children depend on whether we answer the call of RESPONSIBLE FATHERHOOD. We are our daughters' first and most powerful example of manhood. The type of man our daughters choose to date, marry, or bear children is influenced by the example we set as men and, more importantly, the example we set as fathers.

The Epiphany

Dear Gabrielle,

I woke up on Friday, February 7, 2013 with a strong desire to pen a message to you. While at work on Thursday, I learned of tragic news involving the son-in-law of my co-worker. This young father died the night before after suffering an asthma attack. He was under twenty-five years of age, recently engaged, and preparing to move into a new apartment with his future wife and their new born baby. I contemplated his death and attempted to make sense of a promising beginning ending in unexplainable tragedy. Here was a young Black man taking a giant step towards responsible fatherhood and within a blink of an eye his young life is cancelled. His child is now fatherless.

Tragedy awakens our spiritual and moral sensibilities. When tragedy strikes life pauses long enough for us to reflect on our mortality. God does not intend for us to wallow in despair when tragedy happens. He wants us to pray, reflect, and draw spiritual lessons from tragedy. Then we move forward with living, much wiser and with greater gratitude as a result.

As I sat in stop-and-go traffic on this dark and icy evening, I reflected on how the first two years of your life brought so much joy and happiness to my life. I thought about how much I miss you during the day and how I can't wait to see your beautiful face at the end of a long work day. You are such a ray of sunshine; I am blessed to have you as my daughter. When I look at you my mind travels to the future. I think about your first day of school—what will you wear; will you make friends; will you enjoy learning; how will you respond when it is time to leave you in care of your teacher? I think about your first bicycle ride. I imagine you wobbling down tree-lined streets with a huge smile, peddling fast, enjoying the moment in a way only a child could. What about your sixteenth birthday when I am forced to accept "Daddy's Little Butterfly" is a maturing teenager on the cusp of womanhood.

I think about your first date and prom. I pray the values you learn influence the type of young man you *select* to date. I do worry, like any father, you might choose a knucklehead or someone not suitable to my standard ...I am hopeful. I imagine you going off to college. I hope you choose Spelman, Barnard, or Smith—I admit partiality to all-female colleges. I experienced pleasure in meeting graduates from all three schools. I was impressed by their intelligence and self-confidence.

For me, your life is planned. I like to believe things will work out as planned in my mind. In my heart I know life never follows a planned script. There are twist, turns, and unpredictable happenstance and, yes, tragedy we cannot account for when we plan life. Nevertheless, I hold on to faith you will enjoy a life of happiness and meaning. As much as I would like to shield you from unpleasant things in life, I cannot. My hope is to help you develop moral strength to face life with all of its wonders and disappointments. God is the author of human affairs and no matter how much I want to plan your life, I am without power to do so. I pray God bless you with an abundant life marked by health, joy, prosperity, great friends, and tons of laughter and enjoyment.

I am blessed to have spent two wonderful years with you. My heart breaks at thoughts of not having many more years with you. As I reflect on how this young man will never experience the joy of sharing his values with his daughter, I am moved to pen a message to you, sharing my values, thoughts, and ideas on what it means to be a member of our family. My goal is to share with you our core family values and how I expect you to conduct yourself as a self-respecting young lady.

The values shared are not unique. They are influenced by the core family values of the Ellis family, an African American family I read about during my studies of African American history. The Ellis family embodies the best in traditional African American family values. The Ellis parents taught their children love for God and family, respect for education, and an appreciation for lifelong learning and doing one's best. Although both parents were of limited education, all ten children graduated from college, with the majority earning advanced degrees. I desire a similar legacy for our family.

Hopefully you will find our core family values worth sharing with your family when you decide to marry and start a family. I am hopeful... I am prayerful...

Core Value #1

Faith and Commitment to God

୫୦ଓ୫

Core Value #1: Faith and commitment to God is the key to being a successful person.

But if serving the LORD seems undesirable to you, then choose for yourselves this day whom you will serve, whether the gods your ancestors served beyond the Euphrates, or the gods of the Amorites, in whose land you are living. But as for me and my household, we will serve the LORD." -Joshua 24:15

Dear Gabrielle,

Faith and commitment to God is the corner stone of our family. Faith in God is critical to your future success. Each day it is my responsibility to remind you of our special relationship with God. God created all human beings and all human beings trace their origin to God. Do not let anyone tell you or teach you different. Truth will last forever—and permanent values are derived from truth. Deceit—no matter how beautiful the packaging, will perish. Temporary values are like deceit; they are beautifully packaged but ultimately pass away in the end.

Demonstrate a firm belief in God. When faced with obstacles and barriers, demonstrate unconquerable faith, firm commitment, and unwavering courage. Your enemy may win the battle, but you will win the war, if you remain faithful. You will face numerous battles in life. Stay firm in conviction. Righteousness shall always triumph over unrighteousness. Dr. Martin Luther King, Jr. said it best: "The arch of the moral universe is long, but it bends toward justice."[10] In other words, right will win over wrong in the end.

Treat everyone you meet with kindness and respect—even your enemies. People you dislike personally must be given the same kindness and respect.   Doing so will prove difficult at times, as you will meet people underserving of your kindness and respect.   Treat them well anyway. Doing so is a testimony of your faith and commitment to God and proper upbringing.

Show concern for the welfare of people who do not have much. Help those who are struggling. God frowns upon uncaring, greedy, stingy people.   He frowns upon people with a willful disregard for the needs of others. He is equally upset by wasting talent, abusing time, and misusing resources.   Use your talent wisely. Respect time. Never waste money. Talent, time, and money are gifts from God; use all of them wisely. Is there anything worse than wasting talent, abusing time, or misusing resources?

Find a place to worship God. Although I taught you *"God that made the world and all things therein, seeing that He is Lord of heaven and earth, dwelleth not in temples made with hands (Acts 17:24),* attending religious service demonstrates to God your commitment to Him. I must stress this point: God resides in you—a living temple dedicated to the Most High. Find a place to consecrate your dedication to God, fellowship with believers, pay your tithe, and, most importantly, serve those who are without.   Guard your faith and your relationship with God as both are your number one priority in life. Faith and commitment to God is shown by the service you render to those most in need. I believe faith without work is the highest form of hypocrisy. Learn the importance of helping those in need.

Although I am teaching you strict reverence for God, I do not want you "quoting scripture" at every chance. This is a turn off to most people. Do not limit your conversation to discussing religious issues and topics—I am raising you to be a well-balanced young lady, capable of discussing a variety of topics, including religious and spiritual matters. Religious faith is a personal matter; something you need not share openly with friends and neighbors, unless you choose to do so. Your actions, and not what you say you believe, are the greatest indicator of your faith and commitment to God.

You will interact with people who "wear their religion" like an outer garment. Do not follow this example. True religion is spiritual. It finds expression in *how you think, how you act, what you say, and how you say it*. In other words, judge a person's religion by judging how well *"the talk, match the walk."* People love to talk. Watch what they do. Let your actions, not your words, serve as testimony to your faith and commitment to God.

Reflection

_____

_____

_____

_____

_____

_____

core value #2

self-improvement

৪০ৎ

Core Value #2: Self-improvement is the key to getting ahead in a very competitive world.

Train up a child in the way he should go: and when he is old, he/she will not depart from it." ~Proverbs 22:6

Dear Gabrielle,

Get a good, solid education. This is especially important for dealing with critical issues of life. Education is for the purpose of refining thinking, taste, hobbies, interest, likes-and-dislikes, and many other marks of an educated person. Why go to college if it does not refine you as a person? This is why your choice of college is important. I am a firm believer in liberal arts education because it aims to develop the whole person.

Education is supposed to help you gain a better understanding of God, self, and others. It should help you to learn the basics of being a literate person and equip you with thinking skills needed to be a productive member of society. Education should instill a desire for life-long learning and provide a firm foundation for future learning. Education should help in selecting a career and securing necessary skills and qualifications for success in your profession.

Education and professional training are two different things. Your education contributes to living a healthy, meaningful life. Your profession is how you make a living. It is best to choose a profession you find enjoyable. There is nothing worse than choosing a career or job you hate. Doing so is the best way to live a miserable life. Choose wisely as you decide on a career.

Take on the virtue of life-long learning. Use every opportunity to participate in quality learning opportunities; never think you have learned enough. The term "university" is derived from the word "universe." The whole world is your university and it should be used to assist you in learning. There is so much to gain if you stay curious and open-minded. Never let anyone tell you there is something called a "dumb question." All questions are born from a curious mind. Curiosity is the mother of invention and the foundation for innovation. Many "dumb questions" became the next innovation, scientific discovery, invention, or business idea. The only "dumb question" is the question that is never asked. When you are in school sit in the front of the class and ask as many questions needed to satisfy your curiosity. Teachers and professors are paid to answer questions—do not forget this fact.

Although I am a strong advocate of higher education and classify myself a "College Man", do not limit education to what takes place in the classroom, school or at the university. God created us as intelligent human beings. As such, do not attend school like an *empty pitcher waiting for your head to be filled* with facts and information. As an intelligent person, filter and vet information through your own thinking. Let your knowledge of God, innate intelligence, moral values, and desire for truth help you assess information. In this way, you will know whether what is being taught is truth or "deceit" —all things opposite of truth is deceit, no matter how beautiful the packaging. The Bible states: "Beware lest any man spoil you through philosophy and vain deceit" (Colossians, 2:8). In other words, think for yourself and arrive at your own conclusions about things you learn. Dr. Mays said it best: "I would rather go to hell by choice than stumble into heaven following the crowd." [11]

Learn how to stand alone. I would hate to hear you say, "So and so got me in trouble." The best way to disappoint me is to get in trouble following stupid behavior of someone else. If you choose to act stupid, please do so as a "solo act" and not as a member of a group. Be a leader and never a follower; unless you follow a better leader.

Reflection

core value #3

Setting Goals and Working Hard

ༀ

Core Value #3: Always strive for success by setting goals and working hard to meet them.

"Is anything too hard for the Lord?" (Genesis. 18:14)

Dear Gabrielle,

With God's help you will accomplish every goal you seek to attain. But you must be a co-worker with God to be successful in meeting your goals. You cannot work against God; you must work with Him by not wasting youth. When you are young, it is the time to develop habits of success. These are developed by setting small goals and then working towards attaining them. Get in the habit of setting a goal and then working hard to meet it.

Quality of life as an adult depends on the goals set and reached during youth. Remember, the time and energy available to meet goals are limited. One of the greatest follies is to waste time; the other is to waste talent. Learn early to place premium value on time and on how talent is used.

No opportunity lasts forever. Opportunity is like an open door on the verge of shutting. Run through the door while it is yet open. Do not wait for all avenues of opportunity to close before deciding to go after goals and dreams. Set your mind early as to what you hope to accomplish with the time God has given you on this earth.

Your first goal is faith and commitment to God. This is shown through an active spiritual life, commitment to marriage and family, and by serving our community with your time, talent, and resources. Do not become so engrossed in the cares and worries of the world to the point of neglecting your spiritual life.

Your second goal is to be a positive and productive member of our family. You meet this goal by tending to chores and other duties, spending time with family, and doing your share to help and support each other. Never put other things before family. Family is second only to God in importance. Make time for family, no matter how busy you are with school work, friends, professional obligations, and the like.

Your third goal is devote time to self-improvement. This includes exercising and sports-related activities, meditating and self-reflection, reading and writing for pleasure, visiting libraries and museums, playing an instrument, traveling, community service, and other activities beneficial to being a well-balanced person.   Appreciate healthy, wholesome fun. What people describe as fun today is usually unhealthy, immoral, life-threatening, if not criminal. Stay away from activities of this sort. You will live longer by doing so.

Your fourth goal is to excel academically. Being a good student is more than completing class assignments. You need to *"learn the material"*! Why study a topic if you are not really trying to learn it. Doing just *enough to get by* will not help you become an educated person or a competent professional. What you will learn is laziness.

Do not waste time and energy on people, situations, or events unsupportive of your goals. The only desirable energy is energy that moves you forward towards goals. Less productive

energy that promotes standing in place is called lateral energy —
something that does nothing to help you move forward. To
succeed in life you must **"STAY FOCUSED"** on your goals. Get rid
of distracting people, unproductive situations or anything else
standing in the way of your progress.   Read the poem *If* by
Rudyard Kipling. Read closely this section:

> *If you can fill the unforgiving minute*
> *With sixty seconds' worth of distance run,*
> *Yours is the Earth and everything that's in it,*
> *And - which is more - you'll be "a Woman, my Daughter!"*

The "unforgiving minute" refers to the fact every single minute
is only 60 seconds long— no more and no less. So, when the
minute is up, it is gone forever, never to return. Time is not
merciful; it will not slow down as you play or fool around with
your life. Time is not neutral. It will not wait for you to decide
on what to do with your life. Time can be your best friend or
worst enemy.

Fill each minute with 60 seconds worth of hard work and
effort towards meeting your goals. Stay away from wasting time
on frivolous entertainment, distracting pleasures, idleness,
unproductive people, and toxic situations. Throw all your time
and energy on things, people, and events of lasting value. Do not
sacrifice a second of time on foolish, unproductive people. If you
choose to hang out with foolish people, you are communicating
to the world "I am a fool too."

There is a saying: "A fool and his money soon shall part."
It is equally true "A fool and his time shall surely be wasted."

Goals have time limits. Use your time to meet your goals. Don't be an old-fool chasing after a young person's dream.

Reflection

_____

_____

_____

_____

_____

_____

_____

_____

_____

_____

_____

_____

_____

_____

_____

_____

_____

_____

core value #4

Do your best.

৯৭

Core Value #4: Do your best. Let God take care of the rest.

"The Lord your God is gracious and merciful, and will not turn away His face from you, if ye return unto Him."
~2 Chronicles 30:9

Dear Gabrielle,

Do your best. Give 100% effort in all you do. One of my favorite lines is from the movie *The Great Debaters*: "God decides who wins or loses, and not my opponent." [12] I am not interested in how many contests you win or how many awards or medals you bring home. I am not interested in you scoring at the top of your class or earning highest academic honors. I am definitely not interested in how many degrees you earn. I am interested in whether you gave your best effort. I am most interested in you being able to look in the mirror and say, "I did my best" and "I gave my all." If you can do this, even though you may not come in first, second, or third, but last, then you can stand before anyone with chin up, head held high.

Here is a little secret. You are your only competition. Your goal in life is to be a better person than the person you were yesterday; to be better at doing something today you were not as good at doing yesterday. In other words, life is about self-improvement. Don't worry about the next person; worry about yourself. Put all your time and energy into outshining the person you were yesterday. If you do this, you will spend a lifetime growing, developing, and improving. What better than to be a shining example of how doing your best may not always win first place or bring top honors; but how doing your best can earn you self-respect and respect of others. Self-respect is gained when you do your best and let God take care of the rest.

Life can be an obstacle course. You will face many barriers and obstacles on the road to meeting your goals—stay unconquerable through it all. When things get rough—and things will get rough—take a moment to recite the poem *Invictus*. When you recite this poem remember you are in good ccmpany. Nelson Mandela often recited this poem during his over twenty-year imprisonment. Read the poem *Invictus* wren you feel discouraged and want give up or not do your best.

Invictus by William Ernest Henley

Out of the night that covers me,
Black as the Pit from pole to pole,
I thank whatever gods may be
For my unconquerable soul.

In the fell clutch of circumstance
I have not winced nor cried aloud.
Under the bludgeonings of chance
My head is bloody, but unbowed.

Beyond this place of wrath and tears
Looms but the Horror of the shade,
And yet the menace of the years
Finds, and shall find, me unafraid.

It matters not how strait the gate,
How charged with punishments the scroll.
I am the master of my fate:
I am the captain of my soul.

I wish I could shield you from the battle field of life or fight in your place because of my deep love for you. But I can't—you must live your own life, make your own decisions, and decide how you are going to respond when life deals you a "death blow" or attempts to trample you. If you respond with integrity and courage, you will always win.

Moral fortitude will help you successfully meet the challenges of life. With faith and commitment to God, love for family, courage, and *womanly* self-respect, you will overcome any obstacle encountered. Do you trust God? Do you trust me? Do you trust our core family values? If your answer is yes, then move forward and face the challenges of life with chin up, and head held high. You are victorious!!!

Reflection

_____

_____

_____

_____

_____

_____

_____

_____

_____

core value #5

Self-Respect

೮ಂಳ

Core Value #5: To give and get respect you must be a self-respecting person.

Fear God, and keep His commandments: for this is the whole duty of man/woman. ~Ecclesiastes 12:13

Dear Gabrielle,

Be a respectful person. Respect is one of the keys to a successful life. God commands us to be respectful to Him, family, self, and others. Respect for God is demonstrated by praying, trusting in Him alone, following His commandments and scriptures, and by fulfilling the duties He has given you. Remember, your first priority in life is faith and commitment to God. Respect for God requires living a clean, healthy, wholesome life—plain and simple. You cannot say, "I respect God" and engage in certain kinds of activities. You will be looked upon as a "moral tramp," a religious fake, or a hypocrite if you engage in activities contrary to your religious beliefs.

Respect for family is second only to God in importance. This is shown by following our core family values and living the principles found in them. Represent our family in a proud, intelligent, and morally upright way. Family, next to God, is your greatest source of strength, friendship, and support. Do not let anything, or anyone stand between you and the love you have for our family.

Never disrespect family members under any circumstances. There is a special way we resolve conflicts. Never argue to the point of cursing, using hurtful words, or resorting to violence. Respect and dignity is never sacrificed for the sake of winning an argument or to make a point. Long after the conflict is over you have to interact with other members of our family. So, do not say things that inflict lasting wounds. Words hurt! Remember to take 60-seconds to think before speaking.

The crown jewel of life is self-respect. When it is present, life's problems are easy to handle. If self-respect is missing, I guarantee the world will kick you around. How do you show self-respect? It is shown by not engaging in thoughts and behaviors compromising your special relationship with God. And, by not engaging in acts that make you feel bad about yourself or lead to embarrassment if others found out about it. Do not engage in things capable of bringing shame or embarrassment to our family. Remember, you have to stand before God, self, and our family in all things you say and do. Stand upright.

Do not think poorly of yourself. You are intelligent as you are beautiful. There is nothing wrong or flawed about you. Do not let anyone tell you differently. God made you with a brilliant mind, caring soul, cheerful spirit, and beautiful physical appearance. Negative people will try to trick you into believing you are ugly, dumb, stupid, arrogant, immoral, and other undesirable qualities. Ignore them. One of my fraternity brothers has a saying, "You are entitled to your own opinion; but you are not entitled to your own facts." I love this statement! The fact of the matter is God created you to be smart, moral, beautiful, caring, confident, and righteous. God made you this way and no opinion otherwise can alter this fact.

Do not hang around people who make you feel bad about yourself. Negative people practice DECEIT which, as I taught you, is opposite of truth, no matter how beautiful the packaging. Negative people do not like themselves—plain and simple! Pray for them while staying away from them. Avoid interacting with disrespectful people. My advice is to avoid them because they are simply not worth the trouble. Grandpa Jackson would say, "Leave them where you see them."

This is the best advice I can give you. You cannot change negative or disrespectful people—only God can do this. But you can stop being around people who say ugly and unkind things about you or mistreat you. If you are willing to let people insult or abuse you for the sake of friendship, it means you lack self-respect.

If you want respect from others, you must practice giving respect. Treating everyone you meet with dignity, worth, and value—plain and simple. Be courteous, friendly, conversational, and pleasant. Make an honest attempt to make people feel good. But, I must warn you, we live in a very, very disrespectful world where people can be rude, thoughtless, uncaring, and outright cruel. Do not be such a person. I would be sorely disappointed if you were to treat *anyone* with anything other than dignity, worth, and value. Don't try to fit in by acting like a crude, rude disrespectful person. You will fit in with people like this, but you definitely will not fit in with our family.

Here are a few words of caution. While I am teaching you to respect others, I want you to remember—and never forget—RESPECT MUST BE EARNED! It is earned by being a person of integrity, which requires telling the truth. Remember, as I always say, anything opposite of truth is DECEIT, no matter how beautiful the packaging. Telling a lie is disrespectful to God, me, you, our family, and to the victim of your false statement. Truth is the foundation of self-respect; deceit is the underpinning of a "moral tramp." And no one respects a "moral tramp".

Reflection

_____

_____

_____

_____

_____

_____

_____

_____

_____

_____

_____

_____

_____

_____

_____

core value #6

Teamwork

ഇ⊃ ⊂ള

Core Value #6: Teamwork is the key to meeting individual and family goals.

The son of man came not to be ministered unto, but to minister, and to give His life a ransom for many. ~Matthew. 20:28; Mark 10:45

Dear Gabrielle,

Our family is strong and stable because we believe in God and we love each other—plain and simple! Love means sacrifice; it means cooperation and teamwork. We work together on every task. No burden is too heavy when we lift together. We help each other with love, compassion, consideration, and a desire to see each other succeed.

The best way to strengthen family is to work as a team and give mutual support. During the difficult years of slavery and Jim Crow segregation, mutual support is how we survived as a people. Families worked together to feed, clothe, and provide shelter to family members in need. Families pooled their resources open schools, build churches, and open businesses. Simply put, African American families worked together to build strong, stable communities. Our family models these same values of teamwork and mutual support.

At the heart of teamwork and mutual support is love. Stay away from people who do not value and appreciate family. I have a saying, *"Love from one good family is better than the fake-love of a thousand insincere people."* People who love you will to sacrifice to help you in moments of need. People who pretend to love you will disappear at your moment of greatest need.

Do not attempt to buy love or friendship. Both are not for sale. Do not fake membership in someone else's family -to do so is to show disrespect to your family heritage. We have a beautiful family and a wonderful heritage worthy of your love, respect, and admiration. We made it this far as a family because Grandpa Jackson taught us to love God and family over all other things! He taught us the importance of teamwork and mutual support. He taught us to never leave a family member stranded.

You belong to a wonderful community of caring adults who desire nothing less than to see you grow up to be a self-respecting woman. Appreciate associating with like-minded people—people who are positive, productive, stable, wholesome, fun, and great to be around. People like this respect teamwork and mutual support. They will appreciate you and the contributions you make to our community.

Give your best effort to helping whatever team or community you join. Teamwork is a beautiful thing to watch when done right and with the right spirit. I am certain our core family values will equip you to be a great community member!

Reflection

_____

_____

_____

_____

_____

Core Value #7

Laughter and Enjoyment

୫୦୯ଓ

Core Value #7: Laughter and enjoyment allows us to weather the storms of life.

A time to weep, and a time to laugh. ~Ecclesiastes 3:4

Dear Gabrielle,

Laugh and enjoy life. If you take a proper view of life, you will definitely find laughter and enjoyment in each day of living. Although life is thick with thorns and thistles, never let a few of life's prickles rob you of laughter and enjoyment of life's pleasures.

I often wonder why far too few people take time to laugh and genuinely enjoy life. I spent the early years of my youth and adult years struggling to make a living and stressed to complete my education. I was much too focused on making my way in this world to experience a good laugh. Even during rare moments of laughter and enjoyment, I personified Proverbs 14:13: *"Even in laughter the heart is sorrowful."*

Throughout my early adult years, I held on to a false belief the truest end to life is hard work, getting a good education, and securing a profession. I achieved all three but at what expense, I often wonder. It is true life is no idle dream, but a solemn reality. But must life be all somber and no laughter and enjoyment?

Although early ambitions helped me reach the goals I set, it also caused me to miss out on laughter that can be experienced only by spending quality time with family and friends. I missed many joyous moments I can now never recover because, as I warned you, "time, once spent, is gone forever." Never let the cares and worries of the world rob you of laughter and enjoyment. Learn early to strike a balance. Work hard. Laugh hard. Enjoy life.

Learn to laugh with others. Take time to enjoy moments of laughter with family and friends. There is nothing wrong with sharing a moment of laughter with a complete stranger. You both will feel better by enjoying a nice laugh. Laughter is an act of bonding. It cements family ties and strengthens friendships. Laughter disarms enemies, and eases anxieties of new acquaintances.

Life is not one big party. Live a well-balanced life where laughter and enjoyment has its place. Laughter guards against being a bitter, depressed, pessimistic person. Avoid being this type of person. There is nothing worse than being around a person with a permanent frown or a person who finds nothing enjoyable about life.

Life has its share of ill-nature, negative news, and souring disappointments. Life is filled also with amazing people, spirit-enriching events, and sweet successes. Pay more attention to what is good about life. Spend less time harping, complaining, and bemoaning things wrong about life.

Learn to laugh at yourself. Next to prayer, a good soul-stirring laugh is the best remedy for foolish mistakes or for moments when you make an embarrassing blunder. I always say, "Pray on it, laugh it off, and then move forward." You will make silly mistakes and experience your fair share of embarrassing moments. Laugh at your mistakes and awkward moments.

Never laugh at others to be mean. Laughing with someone is different from laughing at someone. There is no humor, joy, or pleasantry in this type of laughter. This type of laughter aims to degrade and humiliate. Never engage in laughter at the expense of another person. Never laugh at matters genuinely serious in nature. There is a time for laughter. There are times when things are not a laughing matter.

Never laugh at yourself when others are seeking to humiliate or degrade you. Never laugh at a cruel or crude joke made about you. Do not play the clown or fool to the delight and laughter of others. Self-respect is lost if you choose to do so.

You will meet negative people who will attempt to degrade you by saying mean things. They will talk negatively about *how you look, how you talk, how you dress, your height, your weight, how you dance, where you live, how you smell, your parents, your family, your education*, and anything else to make you feel bad about yourself. When negative people talk negative about you—and they will, so be prepared—the best response is NO RESPONSE. Negative people love attention. Deprive them of what they desire most: ATTENTION! Stay calm and remain true to who you are as person. Do not show visible anger or frustration. Heaven forbid, do not cry. Stay focused on what is GREAT ABOUT BEING YOU!

Reflection

_____

_____

_____

_____

Bringing It All Together

Dear Gabrielle,

God provides each person with one earthly life. Make your time on earth count for something. Faith and commitment to God is your number one priority. Family is second only to God. Appreciate helping others. Spend plenty of time on self-improvement and furthering your education. Think for yourself and question everything. Set goals and work hard to meet them. Never waste time. Take advantage of your talents. Manage your resources. Do not fear failure. Do your best; let God take care of the rest. Be kind and courteous. Carry yourself with dignity, pride, and womanly self-respect. Respect is earned not freely given. Waste no time on disrespectful people. Learn to lead, and to follow. Never forget the importance of teamwork and mutual support. We achieve more by working together. Associate with like-minded people. Being around great people is how you grow as a person. Ignore or avoid negative people—they are not worth the time or effort required to change them. This work is best left to God. Work hard but do not neglect to laugh and enjoy time with family and friends.

I love you more than you can imagine. I wrote this book of core family values for you. They represent my humble attempt to give you a source of guidance, instruction, correction, warning, hope, and inspiration as you make your way in this world. The world is a wonderful place. Live productively in it. The world is filled also with problems and issues. Face the difficulties of life with courage and faith in God.

Love,
Daddy

self-check

ജ‍�

Self-Check

Core Value #1:
Faith and commitment to God is the key to being a successful person.

I no longer believe in God. Nor do I feel compelled to honor God in my words and deed. I worship things other than God. I have given myself over to vanities, amusements, frivolities and other nonessentials of life. I worship things over God. I value the opinions of others over God's opinion or the opinion of my family.

Core Value #2:
Obtaining knowledge through to self-improvement is the key to getting ahead in a very competitive world.

I no longer seek knowledge or I carry myself like a "know-it-all." I lack curiosity about things or I think I know everything and make judgments about situations, history, and people using my self-proclaimed expertise. I am bored with learning. I do not see a need for self-improvement. I talk vainly with a sense of self-importance that is inconsiderate to the thoughts and opinions of others.

Core Value #3:
Always Strive for success by setting goals and working hard to meet them.

I do not have any goals or I have given up on my goals. I float aimlessly through life wasting time, energy, and resources on things, situations, and people that do not move me closer to my goals. I lack direction and move endlessly from one thing to another without making headway on anything.

Core Value #4:
Do your best. Let God take care of the rest.

I do enough to get by or I don't try at all. I get mad when I don't win or come in first (even when I did not put forth maximum effort). I complain when things don't go my way. I make up excuses on how things are "fixed" or "how people are out to get me."

Core Value #5:
To give and get respect you must be a self-respecting person.

I demand respect but engage in disrespectful and dishonorable behaviors towards self and others. I am incapable of self-reflection. I lack the ability to think about the impact of my actions on others. I accept abuse from others thinking that in some way I deserve to be treated unjustly, unfairly or abusively. I try to buy respect, love or friendship.

Core Value #6:
Teamwork is the key to meeting individual and family goals.

I am interested only in my own success and comfort. I focus on my performance and goals without thinking about the needs of others. I refuse to help others because I see them as competition. I do not value helping anyone unless in some way it benefits me.

Core Value #7:
Laughter and enjoyment allows us to weather the storms of life.

I spend most of my time laughing and having a good time. I usually laugh at the expense of others. I do not find joy in God or family. I use laughter to mask pain or to fool others into believing that I am whole when, in truth, I am broken spiritual and fractured emotionally.

Gabrielle with Daddy

Notes

1. Dr. Martin Luther King, Jr., "Martin Luther King, Jr., Quotable Quotes." Retrieved at: https://www.goodreads.com/quotes/197767-but-today-our-very-survival-depends-on-our-ability-to
2. Ibid.
3. Dr. Robert M. Franklin, *Crisis in the Village: Restoring Hope in African American Comminutes*, (Minneapolis: Fortress Press, 2007), 24.
4. Ibid., 44.
5. Mel, Chatman, *Chandler: The Ellis Family Story*, (2007). Retrieved at: http://ellisfamilystory.com/contents.html
6. Ibid.
7. Ibid.
8. Ibid.
9. Dr. Robert M. Franklin, (Facebook comment in May of 2014)
10. Dr. Martin Luther King, Jr., "Why I am Opposed to the War in Vietnam" (Delivered at Ebenezer Baptist Church on April 30, 1967). Retrieved at: http://www.informationclearinghouse.info/article16183.htm
11. Lawrence Edward Carter, *Walking Integrity: Benjamin Elijah Mays, Mentor to Martin Luther King, Jr.* (Macon: Mercer University Press: 1998), 12.
12. Denzel Washington (Director), and Robert Eisele (Writer), *The Great Debaters* (Film, 2007).

www.ingramcontent.com/pod-product-compliance
Lightning Source LLC
LaVergne TN
LVHW010025070426
835509LV00001B/12